Baby Toys That Build Skills

Other Titles in this Series:

The Wedding Organiser
Wedding Speeches and Jokes
The Best Man's Organiser
The Wedding Gift Organiser
Before Baby Arrives
Your Baby Equipment
Your Baby's Development

Baby Toys That Build Skills

Joan Miller

foulsham
LONDON • NEW YORK • TORONTO • SYDNEY

foulsham
Yeovil Road, Slough, Berkshire, SL1 4JH

ISBN 0-572-01658-1
Copyright © 1991 W. Foulsham & Co. Ltd.

All rights reserved.

The Copyright Act (1956) prohibits (subject to certain very limited exceptions) the making of copies of any copyright work or of a substantial part of such a work, including the making of copies by photocopying or similar process. Written permission to make a copy or copies must therefore normally be obtained from the publisher in advance. It is advisable also to consult the publisher if in any doubt as to the legality of any copying which is to be undertaken.

Photoset by Typesetting Solutions, Slough, Great Britain.
Printed in Great Britain by St. Edmundsbury Press, Bury St. Edmunds.

Contents

Introduction	6
Choosing toys	8
Educational toys and musical instruments	18
Birth to three months	21
Three to six months	27
Six to nine months	31
Nine to twelve months	36
Up to fifteen months	41
Up to eighteen months	49
Up to two years	57
Up to two and a half years	66
Up to three years	78
Up to four years	92
Up to five years	105
Over five years	117
Shopping lists	118

Introduction

Children need toys. Toys are the tools that they use to experiment, to practise new found skills and to learn about the great world around them. They work extremely hard at their toys, and we should help them as much as we possibly can by providing them with the very best tools we can find. Happily the best tools need not be the most expensive. A good toy is a toy that has been carefully chosen with the needs of a particular child at a particular time very much in mind. Every parent knows that a wooden spoon and a saucepan can give infinitely more pleasure than the splendid, and expensive, train set so lovingly chosen by doting grandparents. The toddler will be learning more too — because he is making all that noise all by himself!

Children need people around them too. Parents, grandparents, brothers and sisters are all wonderful big cuddly toys. They can also provide stimulation for a growing child in a way that not even the best toys ever can. People are essential for learning social and communication skills in all their complexity; but people cannot be around all the time, and children need toys as well, in order to learn such skills as manual dexterity, colour differentiation, balance, proportion and so on. Toys can be thought of as learning aids. However, the most important feature of any toy should be that it will provide fun and enjoyment for the user. If it doesn't, no matter how educational or worthy it is, it will stay at the bottom of the toy box, neglected.

This book has been compiled to help you choose toys that will help your child develop various skills, whilst at the same time being fun to play with. Young children learn most of what they need to know subliminally. They pick it up as they go along. This is why the best toys often don't seem to have any useful purpose, but playing with them helps children to develop amazingly well. For example, when we buy a child a ball we don't usually think, 'This toy will help my child to develop hand and eye coordination, will impart a sense of symmetry and balance, encourage an understanding of slope and friction...' It does, though, doesn't it, without us ever saying a word. Certainly not any of those words! The child develops an instinctive, intuitive understanding about a ball.

Although we all want to help our children to develop as many skills as possible, and as quickly as possible, it is important that we let them do it at their own pace. Children have the right to remain young and innocent for several years. We really don't need to make them into scaled-down adults. Make sure your child has some toys that are just fun to play with. Don't only buy toys that will clearly be educating your child all the time. If he really, really wants something that you think has absolutely no merit whatsoever, but you can admit will not actually do any harm, give in occasionally.

Choosing toys

Walk around any toy shop, and marvel at the range of goodies on show. In fact, there are so many that choosing something suitable is often quite difficult, not because of the scarcity but because of the abundance. Where do you start?

It is important not to choose toys purely on their educational merit. Children need some toys that don't seem to have any learning role to offer. They need time just to be. It's the way children have always learnt. They just seem to do it faster nowadays.

It is also important to choose toys for the child, not for yourself. There is no enjoyment for a child in sitting on the settee watching her dad put together an elaborate train set or technical construction kit, or her mum admiring a beautiful but delicate china doll that she is clearly much too young for herself. If you want to buy yourself a train set, go ahead. There's no reason why you shouldn't, and a lot of them are much too sophisticated for children anyway. Just be honest about it. Buy the child a small plastic or wooden one that she can really play with herself. Obviously, there's no harm in buying toys which are just a little bit advanced for your child, and playing with them with her, but do let common sense rule! Nor will your carefully chosen gift be very well received if it cannot be used immediately. A sledge in August, a paddling pool for Christmas or a battery powered toy with no batteries; all will be cast aside.

No one wants to spend money on a toy that is never played with: the money is wasted and the child learns nothing. So, how do you know which of the hundreds of excellent toys suitable for his age group will gain favour with your own child?

A very good starting point for choosing the right toy is with the child for whom it is intended. Watch what catches his eye in friends' houses, and what he goes for at mother and toddler club. With older children you should also listen to what they ask for. But be cautious of the demands inspired by TV advertisements. If your child has tried the toy and still wants it, fine; but these toys can prove to be expensive mistakes. However, nor should you ignore the importance of fashion and being part of the 'in' crowd, even to a three year old. If all his friends have a particular type of plastic dog, then ownership of such a creature may be a serious matter to a young toddler. You may still decide against buying one, but it is not a decision to be made without thought. Also, if you decide to give in, go the whole way; a cheaper version will be worse than nothing!

Another line of thought which can be a great help in making a good choice of toy is to look at your child's problems! Every child has his weak spots, and toys can be enormously helpful in overcoming them. The checklists in later chapters show which toys will help to develop particular skills such as hand and eye coordination or balance. But you can also buy toys to help with minor fears or dislikes. The child who screams at bathtime may be encouraged to enjoy water (even if not the soap) by some new absorbing bath toy. Make sure that the toy is kept firmly for the bath though, otherwise the whole point of the exercise will be lost, and the kitchen will be awash! Night-time fears may be dissolved with a glowing cuddly toy or a musical box. An excess of energy can be worked off on a mini trampoline or a space hopper just as effectively as on you. Using toys for purposes of this sort may require a little extra encouragement from you, but the effort will have been well worth it if your little plan succeeds!

Safety

When your baby is first born, you will probably choose typical baby toys — stuffed, cuddly animals, rattles, teething rings and mobiles. Start as you mean to go on and, even in the most reputable toy shop, don't take safety for granted. Check any toy you buy for a baby or toddler very carefully. Test for example, that eyes and noses are fixed really securely. Check what the toy is stuffed with and what the main body is made of. It should all be on the label. If it isn't, ask the shop assistant. You should make certain that all the material used is new, and that it is flameproof. Foam chips and polyester wadding could both be hazardous to a young baby who could inhale them, so check that the seams are well finished and unlikely to come apart. See if a child might be able to pull off the arms and legs. Don't frighten the staff by destroying all the stock, but do examine carefully before you buy.

If someone else gives your baby a toy, you should check it carefully before you put it where your baby can reach it. Of course, you accept it graciously, but put it at the end of the cot, where baby will not see it. Later, in private, give it the once-over. Hazardous toys are becoming rarer, but no amount of legislation can cover all possibilities. Cheap imports or home-made toys occasionally slip through the net, and young children have been injured by toys that look harmless. It isn't worth the risk.

Find out about the toys you buy or that your child is given. Make up your own checklists. Here are a few questions to start you thinking.

Cuddly toys safety checklist

What is the toy made from?

Is it flammable?

Is it dyed?

If so, what with?

What is it stuffed with?

- Is it made from all new materials?
- How are the eyes and nose fixed?
- Can they be pulled off with reasonable force?
- Does it have ribbons and bells?
- Can the bells be pulled off easily?
- Are there small, removable bits?

Rattle safety checklist

- What is the body made of?
- Is it brittle or will it shatter?
- What makes it rattle?
- Are the bits small?
- How easily can they come out?

Teething rings safety checklist

- What is it made from?
- Is it brittle or will it shatter?
- If there is a chain, will it come undone?
- If it is fluid-filled, what is the fluid?
- How strong is the soft plastic holding the fluid?
- How will it stand up to being cooled frequently?
- Could a baby with teeth bite through it?

Mobiles safety checklist

- How strong is the support?
- How secure is the support?
- Could the moving parts came adrift?

Do not let yourself become any less careful as your baby grows into a toddler — and older. In fact, you need to be even more vigilant as your helpless baby becomes increasingly strong and inclined to throw, bang and pull at his toys. Keep checking all the toys you let your child play with. Obviously, nobody would give a child of three a sharp spike to play with, but consumer groups are frequently warning about dolls with heads that can be pulled off to reveal long metal pins. Similarly, there are dolls with eyes that drop out, soft toys filled with harmful stuffings, toy cars that have sharp edges, liquid-filled toys that contain polluted water.

Most countries have trading standards which are

applied to goods offered for sale, and these filter out most of the potentially hazardous toys, but inevitably a few strays do get through the net.

Of course, different safety standards apply according to how old the child is. A 'young chemist' kit would be suitable for a 12 year old, and we may well expect to find small parts, mildly noxious chemicals and glass tubes inside. This doesn't make the toy unsafe, just unsuitable for children under 12.

Use the following list of questions to help you decide whether a toy is safe for your playroom.

Toy safety questions

Are there any obvious points or edges?

Will any parts pull off easily?

Are eyes, noses, buttons fixed securely?

If it is painted, is the paint guaranteed safe?

For a young child, are there any small parts to swallow?

Is it breakable?

Age suitability

When buying toys, it is very tempting to go for something which is suitable for children who are rather older than the one we have at home. Within reason, this is quite acceptable — but be moderate. There is nothing more disappointing, for giver or receiver, than to find that the carefully chosen gift is years too advanced for the child to play with. Nobody would give a five-year old a full size adult bicycle, so why do we give 100-piece jigsaws to children of 18 months?

The boxes that toys come in often give an indication of the age of child for which the toy is intended. This is usually a general guide, because children develop at different rates. If you can see no good reason why an age limit is applied, ask.

Sometimes a toy which looks ideal for a small child may carry a notice which says 'Not suitable for children under 3'. This is one to take at face value. It is often a safety warning; it could be because there are small parts, or because rough treatment would damage it.

When buying toys, you should be able to see them working. If the shop does not allow customers to take the toys out of the boxes, then ask an assistant to demonstrate them.

If you are buying for a child that you know well, you will be able to decide whether the toy is too simple, or too complicated. If it is a present for a child you do not know well, ask the parents for suggestions. If they have none, or you want it to be a surprise, go to a specialist toy shop and ask for help. Tell the shop assistant the age of the child and the sort of price you have in mind. Ask what the shop's policy is on changing goods. Be guided by the information given on boxes, but check your choice with the assistant, who should be able to tell you whether the toy you have chosen is a big seller, whether there has been any feedback from customers about it, and whether children of the age you are interested in are keen on it. If you are still not sure, try to find a toy that is suitable for an age just a little higher than you want. The parents will probably be flattered, and they can keep it until the child is ready for it.

There are some big brand names that have been around for years. This is because they generally produce good, reliable toys. These companies have their reputation to maintain, so a lot of care and consideration goes into their products. You may feel safer if you go for a toy with a famous brand name.

Don't feel too inhibited by the gender of the child you are buying for. There is no really good reason why boys should not have dolls, or why girls should not have train sets. If you *do* limit them in this way, they are quite likely to embarrass you when they get the chance to play with these 'forbidden' toys at playgroup or friends' houses. Sometimes parents buy what they consider to be acceptable alternatives — what is a 'Batman' action figure but a doll in bat's clothing? The fact of the matter is that young children do not behave like adults; it is no good pretending that they do, and you certainly shouldn't worry if they don't.

All children like to dress up, and will love any costumes they are given. When they start imaginative play they are likely to base it on what goes on at home. They may not have grasped the significance of 'skirts for girls, trousers for boys' yet, so don't panic if they seem to be getting it all wrong. Trying out the different roles is an important part of their growing up.

Finally, just in case the toy you have chosen so carefully turns out to be a real flop, or is identical to the one the same lucky child was given the day before, check that the shop will exchange it if necessary, and keep your receipt. Questions that you could ask when buying a toy for a child you don't know well are listed below, with spaces for you to add your own.

Toy choice checklist

- What age child is this toy for?
- Will you change it if it is not suitable?
- What is it made from?
- Have you sold many of these?
- Will you show me what it does?
- Is it breakable?
- It is guaranteed?
- How long has it been on the market?
- Does the manufacturer have a good reputation?
- Does it need batteries?

_____

_____

_____

_____

_____

_____

_____

_____

When you are buying a toy for a special occasion, such as a birthday or Christmas, allow yourself plenty of time. Start thinking about what you want to get well in advance. At Christmas, this is made easy for you, since toy manufacturers start advertising at prime kiddie-viewing time round about September. If the child you are buying for shows particular interest in a toy, find out about it and make a note of where it can be seen for sale, and what it costs. Remember, though, seeing a group of child actors and actresses playing excitedly with an expensive toy in a glossy tinsel advertisement may not be the best basis for your child to decide whether he really wants the actual toy.

If you are going shopping with a particular toy in mind, have it demonstrated to you and ask if there are similar toys available which might have different features. Some toys date quickly, and children do like to keep in with the fashions, so hesitate about buying expensive 'craze' toys too far in advance. Use the space below to note down features you particularly want to look out for, and price limits that you want to stick to.

Notes

Educational toys and musical instruments

If you walk into any toy shop or look at any toy catalogue, you will find a huge selection of so called 'educational' toys. The purpose of these toys is to help your child to advance more rapidly, to learn the three R's at an earlier age, to tell the time and so forth. The danger is that children may not only fail to learn these tricks — because they are largely irrelevant to a child's needs — but that they will learn to dislike learning. There is a place for educational toys, but they should be handled with care! For example, reading books to your baby with real enjoyment will be far more likely to make him

an early and keen reader than all the letter trays and flash cards in the world. He may learn his letters successfully, and with some pride, at a very tender age. If he enjoys it, then he can be encouraged. But if he does not, don't worry. Reading readiness is a stage that children reach in their own time, when they have the desire to read, and when their awareness of proportion, colour and cause and effect is sufficiently developed. All the toys in the nursery are helping your child towards this moment, just as they are all helping him towards the moment when he will see that 2 plus 3 equals 5, or that lunch will be at one o'clock. Buy educational toys by all means; but make quite sure that they are just as much for fun as any of the other toys in the nursery.

Musical instruments

Babies are born with an in-built sense of rhythm, from the heart beats of their mothers felt in the womb. So, right from the beginning, almost all babies love hearing music and they will join in with great enthusiasm as soon as they can. Musical toys and suitable musical instruments will give your baby lots of fun, and can help develop her natural sense of rhythm into a real musical appreciation. Just one word of warning: do not let yourself become convinced that you have a modern Mozart in the family. The infant prodigy is far less common than the child who has been put off playing a musical instrument for life by over enthusiastic early teaching!

Start off with simple shakers and drums. A plastic bowl and a wooden spoon make an excellent drum kit. A treacle tin containing a few dried peas makes a splendid shaker. (Do not use dried beans because some varieties are highly poisonous until properly cooked.) Put on a tape or the radio, and dance, sing, drum and shake with your baby. At first the rhythm is more important than the melody, and her 'singing' will be quite tuneless. This is quite normal, and remains the case for several years — or in some cases for life! Even children who have absolutely no musical ability will learn a lot from musical activities like this. It helps them to distinguish one sound, or a series of sounds, from the other background noises, which is essential for learning to speak and understand. As your baby grows into a toddler you can encourage her to move to the mood of the music; big, slow and heavy like an elephant, or light and quick like a fairy for example. A little later on you can introduce the idea of high and low notes, stretching and crouching as the music rises and falls.

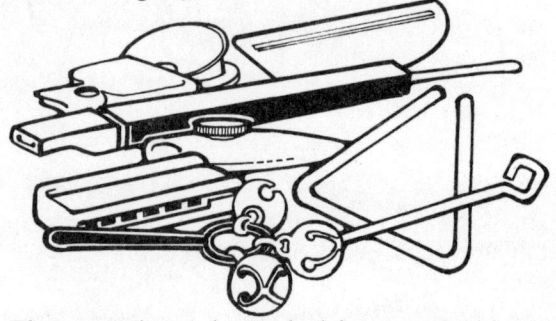

There are lots of wonderful percussion instruments for toddlers, which make a delicious variety of sounds. If you can stand the noise, get a group of three and four year olds together in a percussion band to play along with some tapes. Quite apart from having a wonderful time, they will learn a lot about cooperation! Not until your child is at least four will she be able to make any real sense of a piano (even a toy one) or a recorder. But she can have lots of fun, and learn a lot about music, well before that.

Birth to three months

During the first three months of a baby's life the changes that are seen are amazing. The newborn baby can really do very little for herself. She can hold her head up only for a few wobbly seconds, will cling onto mum's fingers but without really knowing why, will probably not smile except when she has wind, will not shed tears and will spend long periods asleep. By the time she is three months old, she will be able to hold her head up, smile and respond to mum or dad talking to her. She will be shedding real tears. She may spend a lot of time looking a her hands, almost as if she is counting her fingers. This does not necessarily mean she will be a bank manager when she grows up. She has just made an important discovery — bits of her that move. She will probably start to hold things put into her hands. At this stage the baby is changing almost as her parents watch.

Toys that are suitable for a baby of this age include soft cuddly animals, soft plastic toys with baby hand sized projections, big smooth rattles (including those that can be attached to a flat surface by means of a suction pad), rag books and bricks, soft balls and mobiles.

Most soft toys meant for children will probably have recognisable faces. Babies — right from birth — respond to the shape of a human face, and will 'talk' to a teddy which has two eyes, a nose and a mouth in approximately the same places as mum or dad. Make sure that all these faces are friendly smiling ones, and that the toy is pleasantly soft to touch.

Soft plastic toys which are made from flexible material such as vinyl, and come in bright colours, make good presents for babies of this age. Make sure that they have parts which the baby can grasp, for example, the ear of a rabbit or leg of an elephant could be small enough for the baby's hand.

Inevitably, the baby will want to put it in her mouth, so make sure it is easily washable.

Big rattles that can be attached to any hard surface by means of a suction pad can amuse a tiny baby. Of course, any plastic must be shatterproof. If the rattle is put where the baby can knock it with her hand or foot, she will respond to the noise it makes. The same is true of pram rattles, which can be suspended across the front of a pushchair, pram or carrycot. They need to be far enough away from the baby's face so she doesn't hurt herself, but close enough that she can occasionally knock them with her hand. She will start to respond to the noise.

Smaller rattles and teething rings are suitable for the baby to hold, as she develops her ability to grip. Make sure they can't hurt her if she shakes them near her face.

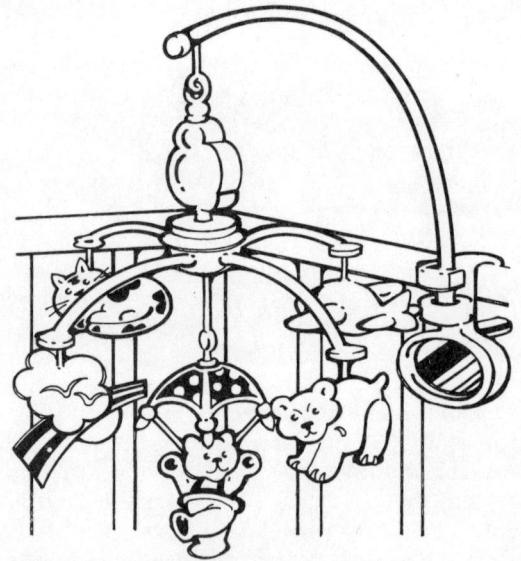

Rag books and bricks are suitable toys for a tiny baby. She can't hurt herself with them, and she gets used to having things around. These familiar toys, close at hand, are very important in the first weeks, as she becomes able to focus her eyes and relate what she sees to what she touches.

Mobiles suspended over the cot or pram will move gently with any air movement. The baby will watch the movement and probably respond by waving arms and legs and 'talking' to them. The following checklist starts with the skills that a baby of this age is developing, and gives you an idea of which toys will help her improve them.

Skills checklist 0-3 months

Face recognition

- [ ] soft toys
- [ ] mobiles

Focusing eyes

- [ ] soft toys
- [ ] mobiles
- [ ] rag books and bricks
- [ ] small rattles
- [ ] soft plastic toys

Holding and gripping

- [ ] soft toys
- [ ] rag books and bricks
- [ ] soft plastic toys

Talking and responding

- [ ] soft toys with faces
- [ ] mobiles

Biting and chewing

- [ ] soft toys
- [ ] soft plastic toys
- [ ] small rattles
- [ ] rag books and bricks

Responding to sound

- [ ] large fixed rattles
- [ ] small rattles
- [ ] pram rattles

An alternative approach is to consider the toys available, and think about the skills they can help build. This will make it even more interesting to watch how your baby reacts to a new toy. Use the following checklists to start you off thinking about toys in this way.

Toys checklist 0-3 months

Soft toys

- [ ] face recognition
- [ ] focusing eyes
- [ ] holding and gripping
- [ ] talking and responding
- [ ] biting and chewing

Soft plastic toys

- [ ] focusing eyes
- [ ] holding and gripping
- [ ] talking and responding
- [ ] biting and chewing

Big smooth rattles

- [ ] focusing eyes
- [ ] holding and gripping
- [ ] responding to sounds

Rag books and bricks

- [ ] focusing eyes
- [ ] holding and gripping
- [ ] biting and chewing

Soft ball

- [ ] focusing eyes
- [ ] holding and gripping
- [ ] biting and chewing

Small rattles

- [ ] focusing eyes
- [ ] holding and gripping

☐ biting and chewing

Mobiles

☐ face recognition

☐ focusing eyes

☐ talking and responding

☐ responding to sound

Do remember that, however many toys your baby has, it will be much more fun if you play with them with him. Apart from any other consideration, unless you make the toy do something, it will remain an uninteresting part of his surroundings. You need to capture your baby's interest and trigger his curiosity about the world around him.

In the period up to three months your baby needs you to do everything for him. He will play with the toys you give him 'by accident', since he won't be able to pick things up or grasp them yet. He may lay and gurgle happily at a pram mobile, but don't expect this to satisfy his every waking moment. He will still spend most of his time asleep, but the times when he is awake and alert are important, since he will be starting to build a relationship with you.

Notes

Three to six months

During these three months the baby may start to sit unaided. He will chew everything and may start teething (look on the lower gums at about 5-6 months). He can recognise his parents and family, but may not be too happy with strangers. He will be able to see toys within his reach, and may stretch and pick them up. He might pass things from hand to hand. He will probably be feeling his feet, putting them to the ground if he is held in a standing position. Soon he will be rolling over, and chattering.

The range of suitable toys is growing. In addition to all the ones he already has, he could start to play with plastic or wooden bricks, rolling toys and simple drums, although he will probably need to be shown what to do. Stacking cups could be introduced, and he is likely to knock them over as fast as someone else builds them up.

To encourage manual dexterity, introduce soft plastic grippable toys, with plenty of baby hand-sized knobs and hollows, such as vinyl balls with cut-outs.

Plastic baby mirrors are fascinating for children at this age. Try to find one with a holey frame, so the baby can grip it easily. A mirror will help your baby to understand his identity as a person quite independent of the others around him. This is particularly important for twins. Study the image in the mirror with your baby and talk to him about his own face.

Simple toys which 'do' things could be suitable, too, such as a ball or roller with a tumbling clown inside, which comes back when it is rolled away.

Below are checklists which summarise the kind of toys which encourage the baby's skills at this stage. Many of them repeat what has gone before, but the way the baby is playing with them is changing now.

Skills checklist 3-6 months

Face recognition

✓	soft toys
✓	plastic mirror

Focusing eyes

✓	mobiles
✓	soft plastic grippable toys
	rag books and bricks
✓	rattles and teething toys
	returning roller or ball

Holding and gripping (manual dexterity)

	soft toys
	soft plastic grippable toys
	rag books and bricks
	rattles and teething toys
	baby mirror
	bricks
	stacking cups
	rolling toys
	returning roller or ball

Talking and responding

✓ baby mirror
✓ soft toys
✓ mobiles
✓ baby bouncer

Biting and chewing

✓ soft plastic grippable toys
✓ rag books and bricks
✓ rattles and teething toys
✓ baby mirror
✓ bricks
✓ stacking cups

Responding to sound

- [✓] rattles and teething toys
- [—] soft plastic squeaking toys
- [ ] drum
- [✓] musical mobiles
- [ ] baby musical boxes
- [✓] baby bouncer

Manipulation

- [ ] rolling toys
- [ ] bricks
- [✓] stacking cups
- [✓] returning roller or ball

Use the space below to make a note of any particular toys which you think have helped your baby with specific skills, or which he seems to like especially.

Notes

Six to nine months

During these months the baby starts to get quite excited about her fingers and toes. She may twiddle her hair and ears. She can probably hold two toys at the same time — one in each hand. She may be able to pick up quite small objects. She probably chatters quite a lot and might even start saying her first words, such as 'Da'. This clearly gives mum the chance to stay in bed all through the night, telling her partner that the baby is calling *him*. If she's got rattles or beads on her cot, she'll have discovered them by now. She can almost certainly sit up by herself, and may be starting to pull herself to her feet, by means of anything she can support herself on. She can probably also move around the floor — or any other surface — on her stomach. She's on the move!

The range of toys that are suitable hasn't changed drastically, but the way she uses them probably has. She can bang two cups together, she may be able to put one on top of another. She may start to throw her toys around the room, then look for them.

She can shake a rattle and may even bang the drum. She is probably ready to be given small toys with moving parts, such as chunky cars with wheels. The returning roller or ball comes into its own, as she can push it for herself and watch it come back.

Use the following checklist to identify the various toys that will be suitable now. Some of them are now encouraging different skills than they were previously.

Skills checklist 6-9 months

Manual dexterity
All the toys listed under this heading for younger babies are still suitable. Your baby will be discovering them for herself now.

☐	soft toys
✓	soft plastic grippable toys (coming into their own now)
✓	rag books and bricks
✓	rattles and teething toys (to make a noise, now)
✓	baby mirror
☐	bricks (she may bang them together)
✓	stacking cups
☐	rolling toys
✓	returning roller or ball (she can now make it work)

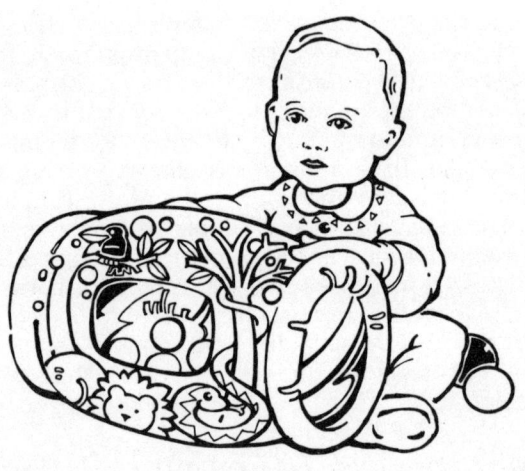

Introduce some new things if you want to.

✓	chunky activity centres (can last up to 3 years)
✓	activity quilts, which squeak, rattle etc

Talking and responding
Your baby will gurgle and chatter quite a lot. The toys she already has will take on new charms.

- [x] baby mirror
- [x] soft toys
- [x] mobiles
- [x] almost anything

New things to introduce include the following

- [x] floating bath toys
- [ ] soft telephone (she'll probably chew it!)

Biting and chewing
Your baby's teeth will be coming through soon, so the old toys may be the best toys!

- [x] soft plastic grippable toys
- [x] rag books and bricks
- [x] rattles and teething toys
- [x] baby mirror
- [ ] bricks
- [x] stacking cups

Introduce a few new things, though.

- [ ] baby cutlery (plastic)
- [ ] baby cup (to get used to)

Responding to sound
The old toys will still be suitable.

- [✓] rattles and teething toys
- [ ] soft plastic squeaking toys
- [ ] drum
- [✓] musical mobiles

Here are some new things to introduce — or new uses for old toys.

- [✓] baby musical boxes that she can start to operate herself — pull strings are far easier than wind-ups
- [✓] stacking cups and bricks (banging them together)

Manipulation
Keep playing with the toys she is used to.

- [ ] rolling toys
- [ ] bricks
- [✓] stacking cups
- [✓] returning ball

Introduce some new things.

- [ ] drum
- [ ] rag books
- [ ] soft plastic squeaking toys

Eye and hand coordination
This is a new skill. Plenty of the toys she already has will help in this area.

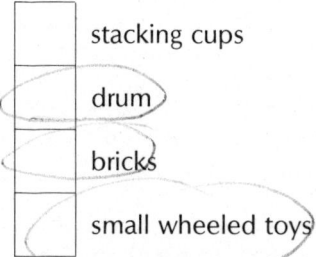

- [ ] stacking cups
- [ ] drum
- [ ] bricks
- [ ] small wheeled toys

Muscular coordination
Encourage the development of this new skill, too.

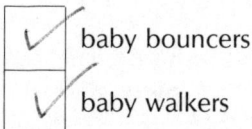

- [x] baby bouncers
- [x] baby walkers

Every baby is different, and toys will appeal in different ways. You could use the space below to make a note of toys which your baby plays with a lot. You may want to keep a record of things that she ignores, too, and look back in a few weeks to see if the old favourites are still popular.

Notes

Nine to twelve months

The baby is probably quite agile, he may crawl and may even start to walk. He can chase a rolling toy around the floor. His memory will be improving and he will probably 'find' a toy that he has watched you hide under a blanket. If he drops a toy, he will know roughly where to look. Mum or dad playing peek-a-boo will make him laugh and chuckle. He may be wary of strangers. He can probably whizz around in a baby walker. He may be getting too big for the baby bouncer. Manual dexterity will be improving, and he probably has finger and thumb precision. He probably has several teeth, so he will continue to chew toys ferociously.

Large, push-along toys could be introduced, but ensure that they are sufficiently heavy and well balanced so that they won't skid away and leave the baby flat on his face. As his walking improves you may be tempted to get a little pull-along dog, train or whatever. It is better to resist this temptation for a while. It is far easier for the unsteady walker to push a toy that he can see and learn to direct, than to pull a toy that keeps tipping over and getting caught on furniture. Frustration will stop your toddler using the toy and his walking skill will not be helped. He might enjoy some sit-and-ride toys though, which will help his leg muscles develop strength and coordination.

Complicated toys such as play-trays or shape fitting games can be introduced, but the baby will only enjoy taking them apart. He may call you to put them back together, so he that can take them apart again.

Use the following checklist to choose suitable toys for your baby as he approaches his first birthday. Notice that some of the items are changing from one application to others, now that your baby's skills are growing.

Skills checklist 9-12 months

Talking and responding

- [x] games with his family and familiar friends
- [x] baby bouncer (if he still fits it)
- [x] baby mirrors
- [ ] growling teddies
- [x] squeaking toys that *he* can make squeak
- [x] musical boxes which he can operate himself

Biting and chewing

- [x] rattles and teething toys
- [x] stacking cups
- [x] baby cutlery
- [x] baby cup
- [x] soft plastic toys

Responding to sound

- [x] musical boxes
- [x] baby walkers
- [x] squeaking toys
- [x] drums
- [x] baby play centres

Manipulation

- [✓] stacking cups
- [✓] drums
- [✓] rolling toys
- [✓] baby cutlery
- [✓] baby cup
- [✓] baby play centres
- [ ] jumbo interlocking bricks

Eye and hand coordination
Continue with old favourites

- [✓] stacking cups
- [✓] baby walkers
- [✓] rolling toys

Introduce something new.

- [✓] baby play centres
- [ ] jumbo interlocking bricks

Memory

- [✓] parents
- [ ] play-trays
- [✓] shape-posting toys
- [✓] rag books
- [✓] card books
- [✓] baby play centres
- [ ] jumbo interlocking bricks

Muscular coordination

- [✓] baby walker
- [✓] rolling toys
- [✓] push-along toys
- [✓] sit-and-ride toys
- [✓] baby play centres
- [ ] jumbo interlocking bricks

Balancing

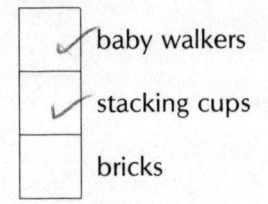

- [x] baby walkers
- [x] stacking cups
- [ ] bricks

Standing and walking

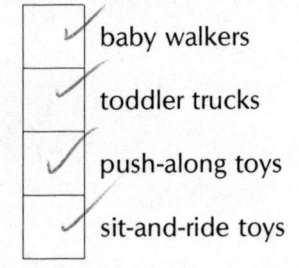

- [x] baby walkers
- [x] toddler trucks
- [x] push-along toys
- [x] sit-and-ride toys

It is often fascinating to watch a group of small children of similar ages playing with their toys, and to notice the different ways in which they play with them. Some children may wave a rattle vigorously in the air, others may bang it on the floor, some may chew it. It is always helpful to see this going on, so that you can reassure yourself that your own baby is not necessarily forward or slow, just different. They all develop at their own pace and a few notes made now can often prove fascinating to look back at in future years.

Notes

Up to fifteen months

Your baby may still be crawling, or she may be walking on her own by now. She will probably have quite a few teeth at the front, and may chew her toys less frequently. She knows her name by now, and responds well to conversation. She may understand several words, and be starting to talk. She may be able to follow instructions, if the mother's body language is sufficiently clear. If she throws toys, it will be with purpose and direction. She may be interested in picture books, especially if mum or dad reads them with her. Colours can be introduced by pointing out the black dog, the white cat, the red box, the blue boat, but she is unlikely to pick them up just yet.

Now that she can sit up by herself and move so much better, bath time takes on a whole new dimension and bath toys will come into their own, bringing lots of fun — and mess! It is important to make enough time for bathing to be properly enjoyed. There is fun to be had, and lots to be learnt in a bath. Finding a slippery bar of soap, for example, combines searching, hand and eye coordination, manual dexterity and lots of conversation.

If the baby is shown how to use a play-tray she will probably watch with interest, and try to help post shapes through matching holes, instead of just taking them apart as she has up to now. With help, she may get some right. She can probably open boxes and get things out.

An activity centre attached to the bars in her cot could be an excellent investment, giving her lots of fun and interest, and you a few more minutes in bed. Don't expect her to play quietly though, so if she's in the same room as you, think twice!

Most babies of this age are very interested in what is going on around them. They are people-watchers, and may become people-mimics. They really do need to be with other people at this age, to gain valuable social skills and learn how to communicate. They will learn to talk and understand what is going on by watching and listening to the familiar people around them.

One of the most important social skills, which is already quite well developed at this age, is humour. Any toy which produces shared laughter and enjoyment will be a huge success. A jack-in-a-box, or any variation on the theme, is always a winner. At first you will operate the toy, and your baby will shriek with laughter and demand that you do it again at once. Later on, your toddler will operate the toy, and demand that you shriek with laughter — over and over and over again.

When your baby is around this age you may want to start using toys to develop specific skills; but this will only work if your baby enjoys playing with the toys you choose. She may by now have very decided preferences, and want to choose which of her toys she will play with. When you buy her a new and exciting toy, she may prefer the box to what is inside. This is disappointing and may be frustrating, but it is perfectly normal. Boxes, large and small can provide hours of fun, and should not be discounted as teaching tools either. A box can teach your baby about shape, volume, hide and seek and physical coordination. It can also, thanks to her developing imagination, be a boat, a car, a table...

Use the following checklist to choose suitable toys. Many of the toys your baby already has are still suitable, although she may use them in slightly different ways. Watch these changes and you will see baby's skills increasing daily.

Skills checklist 12-15 months

Talking and responding
Continue with these

✓	playing with close friends and family members
	growling teddies

✓	squeaking toys
✓	activity centres
✓	picture books
	talking toys

Responding to sound
Continue with these

✓	musical boxes
✓	drum
✓	squeaking toys
	growling teddies

Consider these

	jack-in-the-box
	jingle bells
✓	picture books
✓	clattering pull-along toys

Manipulation
Continue with these

- [x] stacking cups
- [ ] jumbo interlocking bricks
- [ ] play-trays

Consider these

- [ ] picture books
- [x] chunky vinyl vehicles
- [x] building blocks
- [ ] bead frames
- [ ] cotton reels

Eye and hand coordination
Continue with these

- [x] stacking cups
- [ ] jumbo interlocking bricks

Consider these

- [ ] building blocks
- [ ] bead frames
- [ ] cotton reels
- [x] shape-posting toys
- [ ] play-trays

☐ activity trays

Memory
Continue with these

☑ shape-posting toys

☐ play-trays

Consider these

☐ activity trays

☐ picture books

☐ picture cards

Muscular coordination
Continue with these

☑ sit-and-ride toys

☑ push-along cars

Consider these

☑ toddler truck

☐ activity trays

☑ bath activity centres

Balancing
Consider these

☑ sit-and-ride toys

☑ toddler trucks

☐ rocking toys

Standing and walking
Continue with these

- [✓] toddler trucks, with bricks to stabilise
- [✓] sit-and-ride toys
- [✓] baby walkers

Colour differentiation
Consider these

- [✓] stacking cups
- [✓] building blocks
- [ ] cotton reels
- [ ] picture books
- [✓] activity centres
- [✓] shape-matching toys
- [✓] bath toys

Proportion
Continue with these

- [✓] shape-posting toys

Social interaction
Continue with these

- [ ] baby mirrors
- [ ] members of the family
- [ ] picture books

Decision making
Consider these

- [ ] shape-posting toys
- [ ] stacking cups
- [ ] activity centres
- [ ] giant interlocking bricks

Problem solving
Consider these

- [ ] stacking cups
- [ ] play-trays
- [ ] activity trays
- [ ] puzzles
- [ ] shape-posting toys
- [ ] giant interlocking bricks

By the time you baby reaches fifteen months, she is going to be very mobile and surprisingly fast. You can often tell the age of people's children by the height at which they keep their breakables. Parents of very young children — up to about six months — may still have ornaments on coffee tables and TV remote controls on the TV stand. As the children get older, precious things are moved up higher or even locked away. Then, when the children can be trusted not to knock furniture over or scale book cases, everything starts to come down again. It is very likely that your baby is now starting to treat your living room as an adventure playground, so you will need to start thinking about protecting your precious belongings from your little marauder. As far as she is concerned, everything she can reach is just another toy — yours or hers, it makes no difference.

Some of the toys you will be buying for your baby, from now on, can do unbelievable damage to furniture. For example, a toddler with lots of enthusiasm but almost no sense of direction, mounted on her plastic tractor, can dent and scar table legs beyond recognition! When you choose toys, this is a factor which you need to bear in mind. Make sure that there will be space for her to play with the bigger things that you will almost certainly want to buy her.

Think about storage space as well. Large plastic stacking boxes, which you can buy quite reasonably at most do-it-yourself shops, can hold lots of toys and double up as cars or boats when they are empty. They are also useful for carrying all the equipment you need to take whenever you visit friends and relatives.

Notes

Up to eighteen months

Your baby is likely to be walking fairly well now. He may enjoy pushing wheeled toys but is unlikely to understand anything about steering. He thinks that if he carries on pushing long enough, the table will get out of the way. He will, in the end, learn that this is not the case. In the process he will also learn some very important facts about his own strength, and the relative weights and sizes of solid objects. He will probably also have learnt that running into people or animals hurts them, and that running into certain specific objects produces adult anger. These are important lessons, which can comfort you as every table leg in the house gets dented. Quite soon his steering skills will amaze you, as will his speed.

He is probably very active and gets into everything — drawers, cupboards, up the stairs. Now is the time to invest in your baby gate, if you haven't already.

Your baby is developing social skills. You may be able to hold short conversations with him by now. Mothers and fathers can usually understand what the baby is saying, and so can sisters and brothers, although other people may be totally mystified. All toys can help your baby learn to talk, but only if there are adults and older children about who talk to him. The trick is to talk to your baby about his toys, to describe them and what he is doing with them. Keep up a running commentary, ask lots of questions, and answer them along with him. He may understand more than he lets on, usually appearing to have no idea what 'no' means. Don't worry. This continues until he is about 25!

What sort of toys will he need? He's probably getting better at using the ones he's got. The pull-along toys will be coming into their own as your toddler develops his balance enough to glance behind him and still keep going forwards. Give him a box to keep his toys in. To be correct, you will keep his toys in the box. He will tip them out, willy-nilly, and rummage through them. Toys that he doesn't want to play with may be thrown across the room, with amazing accuracy. Learn to catch. Or duck. Keep precious objects out of the way. Your baby will be able to get into everything, and it will be almost impossible to deter him from exercising this new found ability. As a last resort, move into the playpen.

He will be intrigued by toys that do things. Chattering telephones that he can dial, chunky toy pianos, roll-along chiming toys, spinning tops, toys that stick to the side of the bath, floating toys and water-powered toys will all be appreciated. He might like a bead frame, or some pop-link chunky beads. He may be able to help you to match the shapes in simple matching games. Below are lists of toys grouped according to the skills they encourage.

Skills checklist 15-18 months

Talking and responding
Continue with these

- [ ] baby mirrors
- [x] picture books
- [x] squeaking toys
- [ ] games with close friends and members of the family

Consider these

- [x] music cassettes (songs)
- [ ] cartoon videos

Responding to sound
Continue with these

- [ ] growling bears

- [ ] squeaking toys
- [x] musical boxes

Consider these

- [ ] talking toys
- [x] music cassettes (songs)
- [ ] cartoon videos
- [x] musical instruments

Manipulation
Continue with these

- [ ] bead frames
- [x] picture books
- [x] stacking toys

Consider these

- [ ] lift-out puzzles
- [ ] activity trays
- [x] chunky multi-action vehicles

Eye and hand coordination
Continue with these

- [ ] bead frames
- [ ] stacking toys
- [ ] activity trays

He may not be quite ready, but you could introduce these, so he gets used to them.

- [ ] lift-out puzzles
- [ ] giant bead threading toys
- [ ] stickle bricks

Memory
Continue with these

- [ ] activity trays
- [ ] picture books

Consider these

- [ ] stacking toys
- [ ] games with members of the family
- [ ] lift-out puzzles

Muscular coordination
Continue with these

- [x] toddler truck
- [x] sit-and-ride toys
- [x] activity trays
- [x] bath activity centres
- [x] push-along cars

Consider these

- [ ] rocking toys
- [ ] toddler climbing frame

Balancing
Continue with these

- [ ] sit-and-ride toys
- [ ] toddler truck (make sure it won't tip over)

Consider these

- [ ] rocking toys
- [ ] push-along rolling toys
- [ ] toddler climbing frame
- [ ] shuffle-along car

Standing and walking
Continue with these

- [ ] toddler truck (with bricks for stability)

- [ ] sit-and-ride toys
- [ ] baby walkers

Consider these

- [ ] push-along rolling toys
- [ ] shuffle-along car

Colour differentiation
Continue with these

- [ ] stacking cups
- [ ] bead frames
- [ ] building blocks
- [ ] cotton reels
- [ ] picture books
- [ ] shape-matching toys

Consider these

- [ ] giant pop together beads

Proportion
Continue with these

- [ ] shape-posting toys

Consider these

- [ ] lift-out puzzles

Social interaction
Continue with these

- [ ] baby mirrors
- [ ] close friends and members of the family

Consider these

- [ ] other babies (possibly mother and toddler groups)

Decision making
Continue with these

- [ ] shape-posting toys
- [ ] stacking cups
- [ ] activity centres
- [ ] giant interlocking bricks

Consider these

- [ ] lift-out puzzles
- [ ] water activity games
- [ ] toddler climbing frame

Problem solving
Continue with these

- [ ] stacking cups
- [ ] play-trays
- [ ] puzzles

- [ ] shape-posting toys
- [ ] giant interlocking bricks

Consider these

- [ ] picture block puzzles
- [ ] stickle bricks

It is surprising just how quickly babies grow and develop during these months. They will often rediscover old toys, perhaps using them as they were intended for the first time, or finding a completely new and exciting way of playing with them.

Don't expect too much when your baby is put into a group of children of similar ages. They will probably be quite happy to sit together, but are unlikely to start cooperating just yet. Another thing to remember is that they have no inhibitions about helping themselves to other children's toys, even if the other child is playing with them at the time. Although it is horribly embarrassing when your child swipes another child's favourite toy, there is not much you can do to prevent it. Make sure he gives it back as soon as possible, and definitely before you go home if you want to avoid the wrath of other mothers!

Notes

Up to two years

Your baby has probably become a toddler, able to walk quite well, kneel and squat. She may be able to run but tends to crash into furniture. Her range of words will be quite good and her favourite will almost certainly be 'no'. She may like joining in if mum sings nursery rhymes. She will enjoy having stories read to her, and will want to help turn the pages. She may point out things on the pages that interest her. Given the chance, she may well scribble on paper, using chunky crayons that are easy to hold, but her drawings will almost certainly extend beyond the edges of the paper she is given. Watch out for what is underneath her 'work' and, if you don't want murals all over your walls, keep this sort of activity for when you can give her your full attention.

Her manipulative skills will have improved, and she may be able to pile stacking cups or bricks two or three high. She will be getting better at using play-trays and shape-posting toys. She may be able to do four-piece jigsaws — or at least supervise someone else doing them. She may be able to play matching card games. The moment that these games become a real possibility is the moment when many parents are tempted to start 'teaching' their toddlers. Resist the temptation! Jigsaws and the like can be great fun, or a total bore. If they are a total bore they will not get used, and all those lessons in shape, colour and coordination will not be learnt. Start with familiar, easily recognisable scenes in clear, bright colours. At first each piece of the jigsaw should be a whole animal, or other object, that lifts out on its own. Then you can move on to puzzles in which each piece has one recognisable object on it, even if the piece does not follow the shape of the object. This makes it far easier, and more fun, to talk your way through the puzzle, finding, 'the piece with the bell on it', 'the piece with the flower on it' and so on.

Keep it fun, then the game will be played, and the lessons learnt.

Her social skills will be developing, especially if you are able to join a local mother and toddler group. At first she will probably sit among other children but play by herself. Happy cries of 'No! Mine' will echo around the room, while embarrassed mothers smile weakly on. Don't worry! She will eventually learn to share and cooperate.

Your child is coming up for another birthday. You know her well enough to be able to choose her some suitable presents, but use the checklists below if you want to encourage any particular aspect of her development.

Skills checklist 1½-2 years

Talking and responding
Continue with these

- [ ] games with close friends and members of the family.
- [ ] picture books

Consider these

- [ ] cassette song tapes
- [ ] video cartoon tapes
- [ ] talking toys

Manipulation
Continue with these

- [ ] bead frames
- [ ] musical instruments
- [ ] stacking toys

- [ ] simple puzzles
- [ ] activity trays

Consider these

- [ ] jumbo tool kits
- [ ] jumbo interlocking bricks
- [ ] pop-up toys (manually activated)
- [ ] bath toys
- [ ] key-matching toys

Eye and hand coordination
Continue with these

- [ ] bead frames
- [ ] stacking toys
- [ ] simple puzzles
- [ ] activity trays
- [ ] bead threading toys
- [ ] stickle bricks

Consider these

- [ ] shape matching and posting toys
- [ ] jumbo tool kits
- [ ] pop-up toys

- [ ] jumbo interlocking bricks
- [ ] key-matching toys
- [ ] finger crayons

Memory
Continue with these

- [ ] simple puzzles
- [ ] stacking toys
- [ ] activity trays
- [ ] games with members of the family
- [ ] picture books

Consider these

- [ ] cassette song tapes
- [ ] lift-out puzzles
- [ ] pop-up toys
- [ ] key-sorter toys

Muscular coordination
Continue with these

- [ ] toddler truck
- [ ] sit-and-ride toys
- [ ] activity trays
- [ ] bath activity centres

- [ ] push-along cars
- [ ] toddler climbing frame

Consider these

- [ ] jumbo tool kits
- [ ] jumbo interlocking bricks
- [ ] round-bottomed knock down toys
- [ ] lift-out puzzles
- [ ] pop-up toys
- [ ] key-sorter toys

Balancing
Continue with these

- [ ] sit-and-ride toys
- [ ] toddler trucks
- [ ] rocking toys
- [ ] push-along rolling toys

Consider these

- [ ] toddler climbing frame
- [ ] junior trampoline with hand rail

Colour differentiation
Continue with these

- [ ] stacking cups

- [ ] bead frames
- [ ] building blocks
- [ ] cotton reels
- [ ] picture books
- [ ] activity centres
- [ ] shape-matching toys
- [ ] bath toys
- [ ] cartoon videos

Consider these

- [ ] matching card games
- [ ] lift-out puzzles
- [ ] pop-up toys
- [ ] key-sorter toys

Proportion

Continue with these

- [ ] shape-posting toys
- [ ] matching card games

Consider these

- [ ] toddler puzzles
- [ ] floor puzzles
- [ ] picture dominoes

Social interaction
Continue with these

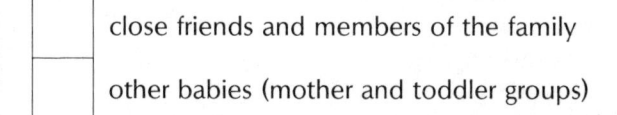

- [ ] close friends and members of the family
- [ ] other babies (mother and toddler groups)

Decision making
Continue with these

- [ ] shape-posting toys
- [ ] stacking cups
- [ ] activity centres
- [ ] giant interlocking bricks
- [ ] water activity games

Consider these

- [ ] lift-out puzzles
- [ ] pop-up toys
- [ ] key-sorter toys
- [ ] toddler puzzles

Problem solving
Continue with these

- [ ] stacking cups
- [ ] play-trays
- [ ] activity trays
- [ ] puzzles
- [ ] shape-posting toys
- [ ] giant interlocking bricks

Consider these

- [ ] stickle bricks
- [ ] lift-out puzzles
- [ ] pop-up toys
- [ ] key-sorter toys
- [ ] toddler puzzles

At the age of two, your baby will probably have a healthy sense of interest in her surroundings, but no sense of danger and little understanding of right and wrong. The good news is that she will be able to understand when you say 'No,' or 'Hot', or 'Come away' or 'Put it back'. You will need to reinforce what you say by your body language, making it quite clear when what she is doing is unacceptable. Social skills are, largely, learnt from the baby's parents and friends. Your baby needs to play with other people to learn how to behave, but the ability to play with children of her own age is still likely to be limited. You can encourage her to understand the principles of 'mine', 'yours', 'his' and 'hers' by playing sorting games with her, although you may need to refer to things as 'mummy's' or 'daddy's' and 'Becky's' rather than 'mine' and 'yours' just yet. This will help when she snatches a bauble from another child, then you can calmly and impressively take it away, saying, 'No, Bobby's' and return it to its rightful owner. If you are lucky, she won't throw a tantrum.

If your baby often seems to want to play with toys that belong to other children, check to see whether it is always the same sort of toy that she goes for. If she always wants to play with other children's giant interlocking bricks, is it because she doesn't have any of her own?

Notes

Up to two and a half years

Your toddler is now likely to be developing skills quickly. He may be able to build towers of stacking cups or bricks up to eight or nine high. He will probably be able to play shape-matching games, such as 'pairs' or 'picture dominoes' properly by now, although his intersest will not stay with the game for more than a few minutes. He will be able to look at the pictures in books, telling himself a story about what is going on. He can turn pages one at a time, so he will know if you are trying to speed up the bedtime story by multiple page turning. Dexterity is improving, and he can probably string and unstring beads easily, and undo simple screw toys. He is getting good at guiding pull along toys, and can manouevre them around furniture. He can probably do this walking backwards, too. He will be getting good at using sit-and-ride toys by himself.

At this age, your child is very inquisitive. He can string simple two and three word sentences together, and understand instructions such as 'pick up teddy and put him in the box'. He will sing along with nursery rhymes, getting quite a few words right. He will listen to stories. He may well play 'action' games by himself, such as giving teddy a tea party or a bath. He will imitate what he sees his family doing and may want to help.

He will enjoy scribbling on paper, and may be developing a sense of colour. He may always use the green crayon, for example. His ability to keep within the edges of the paper will be improving, and he may draw circle shapes.

Activity toys such as cars and trains with wheels which he can move and steer along the ground will please him.

At this age, your child will be able to recognise toys that are associated with specific activities, such as wheelbarrows, dolls' prams or pushchairs, play kitchens, play tools, tea sets, scales, play house cleaning tools, dustpan and brush sets, spinning tops, play centres, shape-sorting toys, jumbo crayons, non-toxic paint (if you dare), floor puzzles. He may also enjoy playing outside, in a sand-pit or paddling pool. The sand could be put in the retired baby bath, or a sturdy paddling pool, and should always be proper play sand, rather than builders' sand, which will turn your toddler and everything he touches bright orange. If you buy a paddling pool and fill it with water, do not take your eyes off your toddler for a second while he is in it.

Persist in trying to keep the toys tidy. Encourage your toddler to help, with requests such as, 'Put the books on the shelf, there,' and 'The bricks go in the truck.' You could try something really ambitious, such as, 'Put the teddy next to the blue rabbit,' and so on. Eventually he will get the idea of putting things away, and with luck this could last until he is about 14, at which time everything you have taught him about tidiness will go out of the window.

There are spaces in the lists below for you to add toys which you notice. The spaces have been left because of the great range and variety of toys available for toddlers. By now, you are becoming your own toy expert and your toddler will be developing his own preferences, so customise these lists for your child.

There may also be some toys listed in the previous section that are not repeated here but that would still be helpful for your child. You should never discount what has gone before as being too babyish: children need constant reinforcement of what they have learnt, and sometimes like to do things that they now find very easy.

Skills checklist 2-2½ years

Talking and responding

	story books
	toy telephones
	baby dolls
	other babies
	family and friends
	_____
	_____

Manipulation

- toy household items
- chunky farm animals
- chunky crayons
- finger paints
- mix-and-match pop-together animals
- advanced activity centres
- jumbo plastic skittles

Eye and hand coordination

- stickle bricks

- [ ] jumbo interlocking bricks
- [ ] jumbo tool kits
- [ ] toy household items
- [ ] chunky farm animals
- [ ] chunky crayons
- [ ] finger paints

- [ ] jumbo plastic skittles
- [ ] sand-pit or tray
- [ ] simple puzzles

☐ bath activity toys

☐ _____

☐ _____

☐ _____

☐ _____

☐ _____

☐ _____

☐ _____

Memory

☐ simple puzzles

☐ card games such as picture dominoes or snap (but don't expect him to do anything more than recognise pictures)

☐ bath activity toys

☐ _____

☐ _____

☐ _____

☐ _____

☐ _____

☐ _____

☐ _____

Muscular coordination

- [ ] big builder construction kits
- [ ] chunky farm animals
- [ ] chunky crayons
- [ ] finger paints
- [ ] sand-pit or tray

- [ ] paddling pool
- [ ] jumbo plastic skittles
- [ ] bath activity toys
- [ ] _____
- [ ] _____
- [ ] _____
- [ ] _____
- [ ] _____

Balancing

☐	jumbo plastic skittles
☐	paddling pool
☐	junior trampoline
☐	kiddie scooter
☐	_____
☐	_____
☐	_____

Colour differentiation

☐	cartoon videos
☐	picture lotto
☐	chunky farm animals
☐	chunky crayons
☐	finger paints
☐	jumbo plastic skittles
☐	picture books
☐	_____
☐	_____
☐	_____

Proportion

- chunky farm animals
- chunky crayons
- finger paints
- sand-pit and sand-pit toys
- puzzles

Social interaction

☐	members of the fmily
☐	other babies (mother and toddler groups)
☐	sand-pit or tray
☐	paddling pool
☐	_____
☐	_____
☐	_____
☐	_____
☐	_____

Decision making

☐	giant interlocking bricks
☐	matching card games
☐	water activity games
☐	chunky crayons
☐	finger paints
☐	toddler puzzles
☐	bath activity toys
☐	_____
☐	_____

Problem solving

- puzzles
- shape-posting toys
- giant interlocking bricks
- matching card games
- sand-pit or tray and sand-pit toys
- water activity toys

Children develop skills at very different rates, depending upon their background and environment, their abilities and their interests. If your child seems a little ahead in some skills or behind in others, don't worry. You may find that your child isn't speaking as well as you would like. If he is second or third — or later — in the family, your problem may be that his brothers and sisters understand him perfectly, so he doesn't need to try. He will eventually make the effort.

It is round about now that all your valiant efforts at persuading your child to mix with other children should start to pay off. Toddlers of this age begin to see each other as possible playmates, rather than playthings. They may start by riding their sit-and-ride toys and banging into each other. What a good job you chose sturdy and safe ones!

You can encourage toddlers to play together by playing with them, as umpire or peace keeper. They may already be prepared to watch a short video together, or listen to a story. You could ask them to fill 'what happens next', and take turns. Choose a matching card game, or shape-posting toy and let them take turns, while you encourage them with suggestions like, 'Do we need a red one?' or 'What about the round blue one?'

When they are used to playing games like this with you, you can start to ease yourself out, still being on hand to help where necessary. You can also encourage them to kick a ball to each other, to teach them to cooperate.

Notes

Up to three years

Your child is probably now quite agile, climbing and running well. She may be able to kick a ball with reasonable success, and she may be able to throw well. If you throw a ball to her, she may catch it, some of the time. Because she can use her hands with so much more skill, this is about the right time to get your toddler a construction kit. Get one that has nice chunky parts which she really can manage for herself. The best kits are based on a simple system which can be used to create any number of different models. Don't worry if your toddler seems to prefer destroying her creations to making them. This is a normal part of learning about cause and effect.

Your toddler will have a far better conscious memory now. She will join in familiar stories and nursery rhymes, and may even supply the endings for you. Picture books are still popular, and she may start putting jigsaw puzzles together by herself. She will probably enjoy matching games such as pairs, snap, picture lotto or dominoes. She may like to look at the cards in a 'happy families' pack, especially if you use animal families which she could sort more easily.

Your toddler's drawing is improving, and she is likely to use large sweeping strokes with crayons or paints. She may ask lots of questions — how, why, what? At about this time your toddler's imaginative play will begin to develop and she may be able to plan a sequence of events, making up a story based on what she knows about. She will probably be keen on the 'props' of these games, such as toy cookers, telephones, wendy houses and so forth.

Her social skills will be improving, and she may sometimes like to play with other children, although her interest span may be fairly short. You could try to introduce the idea of sharing, but at this age the concept is a difficult one. Try not to be too exasperated — imagine how you would feel if you invited a friend in for coffee and then found her rifling through your record collection or rearranging your display of Victorian miniatures.

Persevere with the tidying activities, but make them into games. She will catch on if you are very patient and very persistant.

Use the checklists below to help you choose toys that are suitable. Remember, though, that your child may be a little ahead or behind, so adjust your choices accordingly, and don't abandon any toys you already have in the playroom until your toddler has totally stopped being interested in them.

Skills checklist 2½-3 years

Talking and responding
Continue with these

✓	games with members of the family
✓	cassette song and story tapes (try to find the sort that come with books)
✓	video cartoons and short story tapes

Consider these

✓	let's pretend toys — cooker, wendy house
	baby dolls ?
✓	toy telephones

Your own ideas

	_____
	_____

☐	_____
☐	_____
☐	_____
☐	_____

Manipulation
Continue with these

- ☐ jumbo tool kits
- ☐ jumbo interlocking bricks
- ✓ toy household items
- ☐ big builder construction kits
- ☐ chunky farm animals
- ✓ chunky crayons
- ☐ finger paints

Consider these

- ✓ tea sets
- ✓ pastry sets
- ✓ modelling compound
- ✓ wooden train sets
- ✓ play mats
- ☐ dolls with removable clothes

☐	work bench
✓	musical instruments
☐	number scales

Your own ideas

☐	_____
☐	_____
☐	_____
☐	_____
☐	_____
☐	_____

Eye and hand coordination
Continue with these

☐	stickle bricks
☐	jumbo interlocking bricks
☐	jumbo tool kits
☐	toy household items
☐	big builder construction kits
☐	chunky farm animals
☐	chunky crayons
☐	finger paints

Consider these

- [x] plastic golf clubs
- [x] magnetic fishing game
- [x] simple magnifiers
- [x] play torches
- [ ] scales

Your own ideas

- [ ] _____
- [ ] _____
- [ ] _____
- [ ] _____
- [ ] _____
- [ ] _____

Memory
Continue with these

- [ ] games with members of the family
- [ ] story books
- [ ] cassette song and story tapes

Consider these

- [ ] card games such as pairs, picture dominoes

- [ ] simple puzzles
- [ ] play clock

Your own ideas

- [ ] _____
- [ ] _____
- [ ] _____
- [ ] _____
- [ ] _____
- [ ] _____
- [ ] _____

Muscular coordination
Continue with these

- [ ] sit-and-ride toys
- [ ] rocking toys
- [ ] jumbo tool kits
- [ ] jumbo interlocking bricks
- [ ] big builder construction kits
- [ ] musical instruments
- [ ] chunky crayons
- [ ] finger paints

Consider these

- [ ] mini-trikes or tractors
- [ ] junior slide
- [ ] child's swing
- [ ] space hopper
- [ ] mini go-kart
- [ ] seesaw

Your own ideas

- [ ] _____
- [ ] _____
- [ ] _____
- [ ] _____
- [ ] _____
- [ ] _____

Balancing
Consider these

- [ ] junior stilts
- [ ] climbing frames
- [ ] swings
- [ ] seesaw

- [ ] space hopper
- [ ] trampoline
- [ ] number scales

Your own ideas

- [ ] _____
- [ ] _____
- [ ] _____
- [ ] _____
- [ ] _____
- [ ] _____

Colour differentiation
Continue with these

- [ ] picture books
- [ ] cartoon videos
- [ ] matching card games such as snap or picture lotto
- [ ] chunky crayons
- [ ] finger paints
- [ ] big builder construction kits

Consider these

- [ ] story books

- [ ] dressing-up clothes
- [ ] modelling clay
- [ ] dolls with removable clothes

Your own ideas

- [ ] _____
- [ ] _____
- [ ] _____
- [ ] _____
- [ ] _____
- [ ] _____

Proportion
Continue with these

- [ ] big builder construction kits
- [ ] chunky farm animals
- [ ] chunky crayons
- [ ] finger paints

Consider these

- [ ] various puzzles
- [ ] magnifiers
- [ ] dolls with removable clothes

☐ scales

Your own ideas

☐ _____
☐ _____
☐ _____
☐ _____
☐ _____
☐ _____

Imaginative and creative play
Consider these

☐ chunky crayons

☐ finger paints

☐ infant modelling clay

☐ toy scissors

☐ blackboard and easel

☐ dolls and dolls' clothes

☐ toy prams, pushchairs, lawn mowers, wheel barrows

☐ pedal driven toys

☐ dressing up clothes

☐ story books

	toy telephones
	wendy houses, tents and wigwams
	stick and sock puppets

Your own ideas

	_____
	_____
	_____
	_____
	_____

Social interaction
Consider these

	dolls and dolls' clothes
	toy prams and pushchairs
	toy tea sets

- [ ] dressing up clothes
- [ ] toy telephones
- [ ] wendy houses, tents and wigwams
- [ ] stick and sock puppets
- [ ] simple card games

Your own ideas

- [ ] _____
- [ ] _____
- [ ] _____
- [ ] _____
- [ ] _____
- [ ] _____

Decision making
Continue with these

- [ ] giant interlocking bricks
- [ ] matching card games
- [ ] water activity games
- [ ] big builder construction kits
- [ ] chunky crayons
- [ ] finger paints

☐ blackboard and easel

Consider these

☐ various puzzles

☐ scales

☐ gummed shapes

☐ funny-face kits

Your own ideas

☐ _____
☐ _____
☐ _____
☐ _____
☐ _____
☐ _____

Problem solving
Continue with these

☐ giant interlocking bricks

☐ matching card games

☐ big builder construction kits

Consider these

☐ number scales

☐ magic painting books

☐ funny-face kits

Your own ideas

☐ _____
☐ _____
☐ _____
☐ _____
☐ _____
☐ _____

As you child approaches the age of three, you will probably feel that she is ready to go to a playgroup or nursery regularly, and you may well have had her name down for some months! There, she will discover a whole range of new toys and, as a result, develop new skills. She will also have to learn how to take turns and to share, although not all children may be good at this straight away. You will probably have been putting a good deal of ground work into these skills already, so this is the time to check how your child is doing. Remember that the groups your child will be mixing with now will be bigger than she is used to, which she may need time to adjust to.

Children learn quickly from other children, and they don't always learn the very best skills! Don't despair, you still have a lot of influence to overcome any unfortunate habits she picks up.

Up to four years

Once past the magic age of three, children become much more ready to mix with others of their own age. They usually go readily to playgroup or nursery school, and enjoy playing with friends they meet there. They usually enjoy imaginative play, which becomes increasingly complex.

Instead of simple domestic imitative play, using toy tea sets, gardening tools and so on, to copy adult activities, the pre-school child is able to invent entire worlds around his toy farm, garage or space station. However, while some children will spend hours happily absorbed in their mini world, others never enjoy games of this sort, and there is no point in trying to force them, if it is simply not in their character. Rather than waste a lot of money on a complete toy farm, start by offering your child a few animals, trees and people. You will soon see whether the idea is going to be a winner or not, and if the trees are used as space ships you will also know that you should go for a space station instead of a farm! The props available for play worlds are endless, and range from the very cheap to the very expensive. Your child will learn a lot from either — manipulation, problem solving, memory, talking and many other skills.

Children of this age also enjoy quite complicated games in which each takes the part of a different character, often the traditional family members of mum, gran and so on. They love to dress up to suit their part, but there is a lot more to these games than that. Role playing games are a vital part of growing up because they help children to develop the ability to see things from more than one person's point of view. By dressing up as, and pretending to be, another person the child can explore how that other person might feel in the imagined situation. He can also practise problem solving and tackling disagreements. You should not worry if your son insists on dressing up in skirts and playing the part of mum, he is trying to understand how mums feel and behave, which is very important to his future as an adult man and father. Nor should you worry if children want to 'be' ghosts and monsters. Role playing is an excellent way of working out fears and worries by making them part of the game. A child who has got to have an operation may well insist on playing hospitals. This is not morbid, but a useful way of handling a worry. A child who seems to be for ever in trouble may want to play a role where he is in charge and makes the rules. There is a huge amount for children to learn about themselves and other people, and all they really need is time, and a big box of dressing up clothes.

Their muscular coordination is usually well developed by now, and they can walk and run (backwards and forwards) and climb. Your child could probably manage a small pedal-driven tricycle or similar vehicle. He would enjoy using a climbing frame.

You will need to encourage him to develop manual dexterity. Holding and using crayons and paints helps in this area. If you are brave enough, you could let your child use glue with simple shapes cut from coloured card or paper. He can build up pictures and patterns first, then use a child-safe glue, in a non-spill pen or stick, to fix them in place. If your courage fails you, or for use in bed or at grannie's, you could give him boxes of felt shapes. These come in a variety of themes, and have a flock-covered board to build up the picture on.

Games played with cars or trains on big push-fit tracks will be popular, and those involving simple road layouts with bridges and underpasses are fun.

By now your child may be able to count up to five or ten. He will be able to play simple board games, and matching games such as dominoes, happy families or snap. He may well be amazingly good at memory games such as 'pairs'. Although it is tempting to let him win all the time, it is fairer to let him know right from the start that life isn't like that. Let him take turns, and only let him win most of the time.

Below are the checklists for choosing toys according to skills.

Skills checklist 3½-4 years

Manipulation and eye and hand coordination
Continue with these

- [ ] jumbo tool kits
- [ ] toy household items
- [ ] big builder construction kits
- [ ] chunky farm animals

Consider these

- [ ] finger paints
- [ ] musical instruments
- [ ] play figures and accessories
- [ ] face paints
- [ ] lacing and tying toys
- [ ] magnetic letters and shapes with board
- [ ] junior medical kits
- [x] sponge painting
- [ ] nail tapping board with shapes

☐ sticking shapes

☐ simple magnifier

Your own ideas

☐ _____
☐ _____
☐ _____
☐ _____
☐ _____
☐ _____

Memory
Continue with these

☐ games with members of the family

☐ story books

☐ cassette song and story tapes

☐ simple card games

Consider these

☐ kiddie trumpet

☐ clock puzzles

☐ three-dimensional puzzles

☐ repetitive story books

Your own ideas

☐	_____
☐	_____
☐	_____
☐	_____
☐	_____
☐	_____

Muscular coordination
Continue with these

- ☐ sit-and-ride toys
- ☐ junior trikes or pedal tractor
- ☐ rocking toys
- ☐ jumbo tool kits
- ☐ big builder construction kits
- ☐ chunky crayons
- ☐ finger paints

Consider these

- ☐ garden toys
- ☐ balls
- ☐ simple magnifier

☐ musical instruments

Your own ideas

☐ _____
☐ _____
☐ _____
☐ _____
☐ _____
☐ _____

Colour differentiation
Continue with these

☐ matching card games such as snap or picture lotto
☐ chunky crayons
☐ finger paints
☐ big builder construction kits

Consider these

☐ felt picture kits
☐ face paints
☐ paints and paint brushes
☐ colouring books
☐ construction sets

Your own ideas

☐	_____
☐	_____
☐	_____
☐	_____
☐	_____
☐	_____

Proportion

Continue with these

- ☐ matching card games
- ☐ big builder construction kits
- ☐ chunky farm animals
- ☐ magnifiers

Consider these

- ☐ tool kits
- ☐ play figures and accessories
- ☐ paper shapes
- ☐ plastic scissors
- ☐ felt shape kits

Your own ideas

☐	_____
☐	_____
☐	_____
☐	_____
☐	_____
☐	_____

Imaginative and creative play
Continue with these

- ☐ chunky crayons
- ☐ finger paints
- ☐ infant modelling clay
- ☐ toy scissors
- ☐ blackboard and easel
- ☐ dolls and dolls' clothes
- ☐ toy prams, pushchairs, lawn mowers
- ☐ pedal-driven toys
- ☐ dressing up clothes
- ☐ story books
- ☐ toy telephones

- [ ] wendy houses, tents and wigwams
- [ ] stick and sock puppets

Consider these

- [ ] felt shape kits
- [ ] musical instruments
- [ ] three-dimensional pop-together shapes

Your own ideas

- [ ] _____
- [ ] _____
- [ ] _____
- [ ] _____
- [ ] _____
- [ ] _____

Social interaction
Continue with these

- [ ] dolls and dolls' clothes
- [ ] toy prams and pushchairs
- [ ] pedal-driven toys
- [ ] dressing up clothes
- [ ] toy telephones

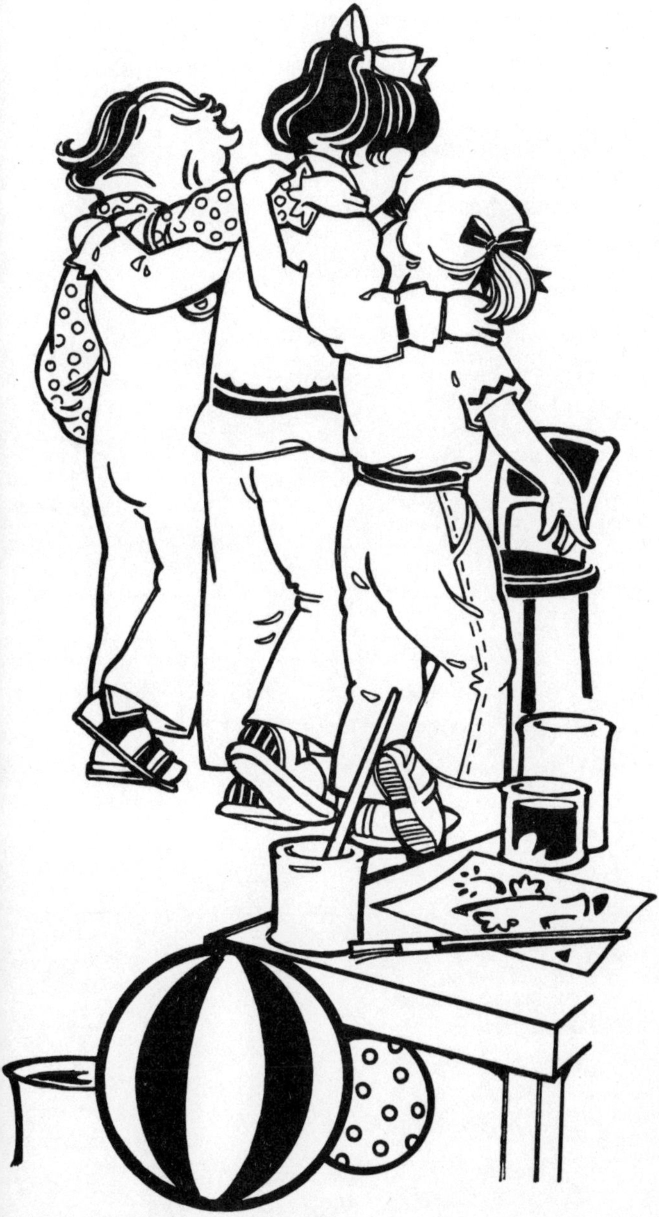

- [ ] wendy houses, tents and wigwams
- [ ] stick and sock puppets
- [ ] simple card games
- [ ] simple board games

Consider these

- [ ] simple interactive games
- [ ] kiddie slides (taking turns)
- [ ] ball games
- [ ] kiddie shops

Your own ideas

- [ ] _____
- [ ] _____
- [ ] _____
- [ ] _____
- [ ] _____
- [ ] _____

Decision making and problem solving
Continue with these

- matching card games
- big builder construction kits
- chunky crayons
- finger paints
- blackboard and easel

Consider these

- kiddie shops
- simple interactive games
- ball games
- simple board games
- clock puzzles

Your own ideas

- _____
- _____
- _____
- _____
- _____
- _____

Buying toys for your child should be getting easier now, since his likes and dislikes are becoming quite distinct. This doesn't mean that you should always stick to the same type of toy, though. Include some surprises and see how they go down. Watch your child as he plays, and see if you can spot any areas where you think he needs encouragement. You may even notice special talents that could be developed, too. Do remember, though, that at four life should be fun, and it is your child's right to be able to play happily without being pestered to improve himself. Try to balance your eager encouragement with plenty of times when he can choose what to do for himself. It is still very important that you spend plenty of time with your child, and your company is really the best thing you can give him.

There is space below for you to make notes about what sort of toys you think your child could benefit from, so next time someone offers a present you will have ideas at your fingertips.

Notes

Up to five years

This is it! The run up to school. In the UK, children start school at the latest in the term that they will be five years old.

Your child's speech will be fluent, and she will be able to put together quite complicated sentences. She will be able to hold a conversation, and describe what she has been doing with considerable imagination and accuracy. She may be developing a sense of humour. She may make up imaginary friends, and use her own made-up words if there is something just outside her vocabulary. She may say, for example, 'Natasha bees horrid'. If you correct her, saying, 'No, dear, Natasha is horrid,' she will know, and tell you, that that isn't what she means at all. What she is trying to express is the fact that sometimes Natasha can be quite a little madam, but most of the time she is her best friend.

Your child will be energetic and agile. She will be learning to stand on one leg, and to hop. She may be ready for a bicycle, starting with stabilisers. The climbing frame will be a great source of fun (and of anxiety for watching parents). You may already have enrolled her in swimming lessons, or be teaching her to ice-skate. Her sense of balance will be good, and she will probably run along the top of low walls quite easily.

By now your child will have developed a tendency towards being left or right-handed. She will probably be drawing recognisable shapes, such as faces and houses. She will be able to add stick arms and legs to pictures of mum and dad, and the features will be in the right places. She will probably give a fair indication of hair colour and style too. Although freehand drawing will be good, she still won't be able to colour inside lines of predrawn pictures. Providing colouring books could encourage her in this area. They also help with shape recognition and colour coordination.

Choose toys that will encourage her in all the skills that she will need for school, since her teacher will have up to thirty tiny children in her charge and won't have time to tie 60 shoelaces. She may be able to copy her name, and draw letter and number shapes. It will be more important though, to make sure that she can take off and put on her own coat and shoes.

Skills checklist 4-5 years

Talking and responding
Continue with these

- [ ] cassette and video tapes
- [ ] story books

Consider these

- [ ] interactive story books
- [ ] cassette recorder
- [ ] speak and spell toys
- [ ] play and say toys
- [ ] counting puzzles

Your own ideas

- [ ] _____
- [ ] _____
- [ ] _____
- [ ] _____

☐ _____
☐ _____

Manipulation
Continue with these

☐ jumbo tool kits

☐ toy household items

☐ big builder construction kits

Consider these

☐ medium-sized interlocking bricks

☐ cassette recorders

☐ simple technical construction kits

☐ magnetic letters and numbers

☐ chalk and blackboard

☐ seed planting kits

☐ musical instruments such as recorder

☐ simple slot racing tracks

Your own ideas

☐ _____
☐ _____
☐ _____

☐ _____
☐ _____
☐ _____

Eye and hand coordination
Continue with these

☐ toy household items

☐ big builder construction kits

☐ chunky crayons

☐ finger paints

Consider these

☐ medium-sized interlocking bricks

☐ scales

☐ pantograph

☐ sand and water trays

☐ junior meccano

☐ simple tracing books

☐ peg mosaic boards

Your own ideas

☐ _____
☐ _____

☐ _____
☐ _____
☐ _____
☐ _____

Memory
Continue with these

☐ story books

☐ cassette song and story tapes

☐ card games and board games

Consider these

☐ counting games

☐ spelling games

☐ letter recognition games

☐ children's poetry books

Your own ideas

☐ _____
☐ _____
☐ _____
☐ _____
☐ _____
☐ _____

Muscular coordination
Continue with these

- [ ] pedal-driven toys
- [ ] jumbo tool kits
- [ ] big builder construction kits
- [ ] chunky crayons
- [ ] finger paints

Consider these

- [ ] medium-sized interlocking bricks
- [ ] junior meccano
- [ ] bicycle with stabilisers
- [ ] ball games such as croquet
- [ ] roller skates
- [ ] sand tray, bucket and spade
- [ ] plastic stilts

Your own ideas

- [ ] _____
- [ ] _____
- [ ] _____
- [ ] _____

| | _____ |
| | _____ |

Imaginative and creative play, colour and proportion
Continue with these

- [ ] chunky crayons
- [ ] finger paints
- [ ] infant modelling compound
- [ ] blackboard and easel
- [ ] doll and dolls' clothes
- [ ] toy prams, pushchairs, lawn mowers and wheel barrows
- [ ] pedal-driven toys
- [ ] dressing up clothes
- [ ] story books
- [ ] toy telephones
- [ ] wendy houses, tents and wigwams
- [ ] stick and sock puppets
- [ ] felt shape kits

Consider these

- [ ] kaleidoscope
- [ ] masks

- [ ] scales
- [ ] sand tray, bucket and spade
- [ ] junior meccano
- [ ] painting templates
- [ ] art packs such as collage kits, artstraws
- [ ] Christmas card colouring kits
- [ ] mosaic picture making kit
- [ ] pantograph

Your own ideas

- [ ] _____
- [ ] _____
- [ ] _____
- [ ] _____
- [ ] _____
- [ ] _____

Social interaction
Continue with these

- [ ] dolls and dolls' clothes
- [ ] toy prams and pushchairs
- [ ] pedal-driven toys

- [ ] dressing up clothes
- [ ] toy telephones
- [ ] wendy houses, tents and wigwams
- [ ] stick and sock puppets

Consider these

- [ ] simple card games
- [ ] ball games such as croquet
- [ ] simple board games
- [ ] jumbo cricket set
- [ ] junior walkie-talkie set

Your own ideas

- [ ] _____
- [ ] _____
- [ ] _____
- [ ] _____
- [ ] _____
- [ ] _____

Decision making
Continue with these

- [ ] matching card games

- [ ] big builder construction kits
- [ ] chunky crayons
- [ ] finger paints
- [ ] blackboard and easel

Consider these

- [ ] junior meccano
- [ ] ball games
- [ ] board games
- [ ] card games
- [ ] interactive story books
- [ ] seed planting kits
- [ ] scrap books
- [ ] simple hobby and collector kits

Your own ideas

- [ ] _____
- [ ] _____
- [ ] _____
- [ ] _____
- [ ] _____
- [ ] _____

Problem solving
Continue with these

- [ ] matching card games
- [ ] big builder construction kits

Consider these

- [ ] ball games
- [ ] interactive story books
- [ ] medium-sized interlocking bricks
- [ ] puzzles
- [ ] kites
- [ ] hobby kits

Your own ideas

- [ ] _____
- [ ] _____
- [ ] _____
- [ ] _____
- [ ] _____
- [ ] _____
- [ ] _____
- [ ] _____

It is often a wrench when your child — your constant companion for almost five years, and your pride and joy — leaves to go to school. Suddenly there is someone else in his life, whom he adores and calls 'Miss' or 'My Teacher'. Don't worry, this will probably only last for about a term, after which time he will be sufficiently used to his new surroundings to turn his attention increasingly towards friends of his own age.

At about the same time, your child will become a toy connoisseur, exchanging opinions and ideas with his class mates. Now is the time when you will really have to be on your toes if you want to keep up to date with what toys are in and what are out. Many 'new' board games become popular, although they may appear to you to be just like what you had at the same age, painted different colours. Crazes, often related to popular TV shows or films, sweep through the country; don't rush to buy them straight away, since some of them just don't make it. If there is something which your child keeps mentioning, make a note of it in the space below. If he is still talking about it in three or four weeks, it might be just what you are looking for for his next birthday or Christmas present.

Notes

Over five years

Although by the age of five most children have grasped the basics of most skills they need for life, there is still plenty of room for improvement.

Once a child starts school, he begins to develop his own interests and hobbies. Of course, this is as it should be, because however broad the interests of the parents are, nobody can know everything about everything. You can encourage your child to take full advantage of any facilities and opportunities that are offered. There may be extra-curricular activities such as hobby clubs and special interest outings. Your child may want to join one of the youth organisations which aim to encourage individuality and self-confidence. He may want to take up music or dancing.

So how do you choose toys for children over five? Basically the same way as before, but now you have to be aware of their special interests and hobbies. If your son loves football but you don't, buying him a stamp-collecting kit won't necessarily diminish his passion for the game. It might give him a second consuming interest though, especially if you are interested too, and give him lots of encouragement.

Try to keep your child's range of interests broad. You can do this by buying him a hobby starter kit on one topic, getting him a book about another, and taking him to an exhibition about a third and so on. Needless to say, he will not enjoy any of them unless you join in and show enthusiasm too.

On the next pages are shopping lists, which you can use to help you decide upon the type of presents you want to buy for your child as he grows up.

Shopping lists

Use these lists to identify what toy to buy for your child, or anyone else's. Make a note of the age and sex of the child at the time and the price you want to pay. Write down any particular skills you want to encourage in the child. Then you can make a list of suitable toys. When you go to the shop you can use your list to prepare a shortlist, before finally deciding what to buy.

You can also use these pages to keep a useful record of what you have given each child over the years. You can note down how the child used the toy, giving you a fascinating insight into her development at each age, in the years to come.

Shopping list   Date _____

- name of child   _____
- age of child   _____
- reason for giving   _____
- price range   _____
- skills   _____

_____

_____

_____

_____

toy suggestions

Shortlist

Model	Brand	Price	Bought
_____	_____	_____	
_____	_____	_____	
_____	_____	_____	
_____	_____	_____	

Comments

Shopping list

Date _____

- name of child
- age of child
- reason for giving
- price range
- skills

toy suggestions

Shortlist

Model	Brand	Price	Bought
_____	_____	_____	
_____	_____	_____	
_____	_____	_____	
_____	_____	_____	

Comments

_____
_____
_____
_____
_____
_____

Shopping list   Date _____

- name of child   _____
- age of child   _____
- reason for giving   _____
- price range   _____

skills   _____

                                    _____

                                    _____

                                    _____

                                    _____

toy suggestions   _____

                                    _____

                                    _____

                                    _____

                                    _____

                                    _____

Shortlist

Model	Brand	Price	Bought
_____	_____	_____	
_____	_____	_____	
_____	_____	_____	
_____	_____	_____	

Comments

_____

_____

_____

_____

_____

_____

Shopping list   Date _____

- name of child   _____
- age of child   _____
- reason for giving   _____
- price range   _____
- skills   _____

_____

_____

_____

_____

toy suggestions   _____

Shortlist

Model	Brand	Price	Bought

Comments

Shopping list

Date _____

- name of child
- age of child
- reason for giving
- price range
- skills

toy suggestions

Shortlist

Model	Brand	Price	Bought
_____	_____	_____	
_____	_____	_____	
_____	_____	_____	
_____	_____	_____	

Comments

_____
_____
_____
_____
_____
_____

Shopping list   Date _____

- name of child   _____
- age of child   _____
- reason for giving   _____
- price range   _____

skills

toy suggestions

Shortlist

Model	Brand	Price	Bought
_____	_____	_____	
_____	_____	_____	
_____	_____	_____	
_____	_____	_____	

Comments

_____

_____

_____

_____

_____

_____

And finally . . .

Having watched your child develop over the last five years, you will probably have been fascinated to see what toys she fell on with delight, what toys went everywhere with their young owner, and what was left determindly at the bottom of the toybox, neglected. You will probably have made a few mistakes, but we hope that these were *very* few. If any toys were especially successful (or even unsuccessful!) it could be useful to make a note of them, below, for future reference. After all, if you have children now, you may have grandchildren some time in the future.

Buying toys for children, even those you know well, can often be a chancy occupation, but we hope that this book has helped in some ways. If nothing else, buying toys does offer the opportunity of visiting toy departments and shops and, briefly, recapturing those days when you could be anything you wanted and all you needed was the imagination . . .

Notes